A Day in the Life of a Colonial Sea Captain

J. L. Branse

The Rosen Publishing Group's
PowerKids Press ™
New York

For my mother, who always keeps me on course

Published in 2002 by The Rosen Publishing Group, Inc.
29 East 21st Street, New York, NY 10010

First Edition

Book Design: Danielle Primiceri
Layout Design: Maria E. Melendez
Project Editor: Frances E. Ruffin

Photo Credits: Cover and title page, (portrait of a sea captain) © Francis G. Mayer/CORBIS; p. 4 (an old whaler under sail), p. 7 (view of Nantucket, MA, 1850s), p. 8 ("There she blows" cry of whaling ship lookout, 1800s), p. 12 (sperm whale aground, 1800s), p. 12 (right whale spouting), p. 15 (rig on whaling schooner with lookout calling "There sh' blows"), p. 19 (attacking whale), p. 20 (angry whale chasing harpoon boat) © North Wind Pictures; p. 11 (carving scrimshaw) © Kelly-Mooney Photography/CORBIS; p. 16 (attacking whale with hand harpo) © Bettmann/CORBIS.

Branse, J. L..
    A day in the life of a colonial sea captain / J. L. Branse.—1st ed.
        p. cm. — (The library of living and working in colonial times)
Includes index.
    ISBN 0-8239-5821-3
    1. Whaling—United States—History—18th century—Juvenile literature. 2. Whalers (Persons)—United States—History—18th century—Juvenile literature. I. Title. II. Series.
SH381.5 .B73 2002
639.2'8'097309033—dc21   00-012301

Contents

Captain Burke

On a fall day in 1770, Captain Charles Burke sat in his cabin on the whaling ship *Christina*. Burke was worried that the men under his command were growing restless. Nearly a month before, the *Christina* had left Nantucket, an island in Massachusetts, to hunt whales all the way to South America. No whales had been spotted yet, however. Today we understand that it is wrong to hunt whales, but in **colonial** times they were prized for their oil. Oil made from a whale's **blubber** had many uses in the eighteenth century.

◄ *Whaling ships were used to hunt whales for their oil. Whale oil was used in lamps, for making candles, and as a lubricant.*

Born a Sailor

Charles Burke had been on many whaling **voyages**, but this was his first time as captain. He knew he had to prove himself to his **crew**. Burke also wanted to make a good living for his wife, Faith, and two daughters. Charles and Faith were born on Nantucket Island. The people of Nantucket were **Quakers**. They did not believe in war. Most of the men hunted whales, however, and considered it honest work. When English **settlers** came to Nantucket in the 1600s, Native Americans taught them how to hunt whales.

Whaling was an important industry for the people of Nantucket Island for almost two hundred years. ▶

On the Lookout

Captain Charles Burke walked the **deck** of the whaling ship *Christina*. He said hello to the cabin boy, whose job was to sweep the decks and make sure that the lines from the ship's sails were **coiled** tightly. At 30 years old, Captain Burke remembered his time as a cabin boy when he was a teenager. Cabin boys often were on their first sea voyage and were treated roughly by the other sailors. Burke was seasick during his first few days at sea. Sick or not, he had to climb up the **mast** of the ship to see if he could spot a whale.

◀ The man in the picture is a lookout. It is the lookout's job to climb the main mast of a whaling ship to spot whales.

Dangers at Sea

Every two hours, a different man went up the mast. Burke saw that the lookout coming down the mast was Marcus Wallace. Wallace was a neighbor from Nantucket. His father had been killed on a whaling ship. Whalers faced many dangers at sea. A sailor could get tossed overboard during a storm, die of an illness, or be killed by a whale while hunting it. Like his father, Marcus Wallace was a brave sailor. He also was very good at scrimshaw. This was the art of **engraving** pictures and sayings onto whale teeth.

Sailors carved scrimshaw onto whale teeth to help pass the time during their long hours at sea. ▶

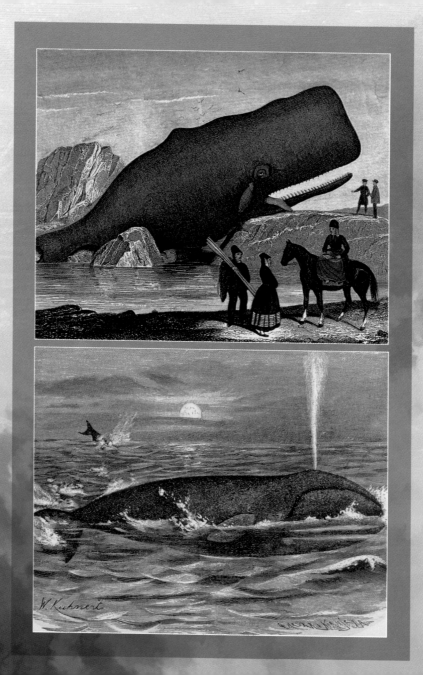

W. Kuhnert

Sperm Whales and Right Whales

Captain Burke and his men were hunting a type of whale called a sperm whale. Its blubber produced oil that burned very cleanly and brightly. Sperm whales were not the only whales Nantucket men had ever hunted. Captain Burke's father and grandfather had hunted right whales that swam close to the shores of Nantucket. These whales got their name because the whalers said they were the "right whale" to kill. They killed so many of these whales, however, that by the mid-1700s there were almost no right whales anymore.

◄ *Whalers had to travel far from home, and for many months, to find sperm whales* (top) *and right whales* (bottom).

"There She Blows!"

In the early afternoon, Captain Burke and Jarrod Cooke, his **first mate**, heard a man call out, "There she blows!" The lookout, at the top of the main mast, had spotted a whale. Captain Burke and the first mate rushed to the deck of the ship. The *Christina* carried two smaller rowboats called whaleboats. Burke and Jarrod Cooke were each in charge of a boat. The two men had already chosen the crew they would take with them in their boat. Burke was glad that he did not have any "**green hands**" in his whaleboat.

Once the lookout shouted, "There she blows!" the men on a large whaler jumped into small whaleboats. ▶

Setting Out

The crew of the *Christina* lowered two whaleboats into the Atlantic Ocean. Two men, called shipkeepers, stayed behind and watched over the *Christina*. Four **oarsmen** were in each whaleboat with either Captain Burke or the first mate. A man called the boatsteerer sat at the front of the boat. When a whaleboat caught up with a whale, the boatsteerer caught the whale with a **harpoon**. This would slow it down just enough to let the men attach their small boat to the animal using a thick wire called a whale-line.

◀ *The scene shows a whale being approached by two whaleboats. A large whaler ship is in the background.*

The Chase

The five men in Captain Burke's whaleboat rowed hard as they tried to catch up with the sperm whale. Burke and his men were preparing to attack an animal that was about 60 feet (18 m) long and weighed more than 40 tons (36 t). The whale also had many sharp teeth in its huge and powerful jaw. The first mate's boat was pulling ahead. Burke called to his men to row harder. With a few final pulls, Burke's boat took the lead. The whale was theirs to catch.

If an angry whale came up under a whaleboat, it could crack it in half, or knock all of the men into the Atlantic. ▶

A Whale Is Captured

Marcus Wallace, the boatsteerer, hooked the whale with a harpoon. The boat was now attached to the animal by the whale-line. The whale fought to get away, racing along the Atlantic and taking the boat with it. Captain Burke moved to the front of the boat to be near the whale. When a whale tired, the men used the whale-line to pull themselves close to it. The captain was the man who killed the whale. This was seen as an honor, though we now know that hunting whales is a **cruel** practice.

◄ *A wounded, angry whale often attacked its hunters before it was killed.*

The Struggle Ends

The men in the boat struck at the whale. The whale swam in tighter and tighter circles until it finally died. Captain Burke did not enjoy seeing the life go out of this creature. Once a whale was killed, it had to be attached to the boat and rowed back. This was a tiring job. The men could not row fast towing a whale. It would likely be dark by the time that Burke, his men, and the whale got back to the *Christina*. On a whaling ship, there was always much work to do. It was the captain's job to make sure that the work went smoothly.

Glossary

blubber (BLUH-ber) The fat of a whale, penguin, or other sea animal.

coiled (KOYLD) Twisted into rings.

colonial (kuh-LOH-nee-ul) The period of time when the United States was made up of thirteen colonies, ruled by England.

crew (KROO) The men who work for the officers on a ship.

cruel (KROOL) Very mean.

deck (DEK) The floor of a ship.

engraving (en-GRAY-ving) Cutting a picture into wood, stone, or other materials.

first mate (FURST MAYT) The officer on a ship who ranks right below the captain.

green hands (GREEN HANDZ) Nantucket term for new sailors.

harpoon (har-POON) A blade used to hunt large fish or whales.

mast (MAST) A long pole that holds up the sail of a ship.

oarsmen (ORZ-min) The men who row a boat.

Quakers (KWAY-kurz) People who belong to a religion that believes in equality for all people, strong families and communities, and peace.

settlers (SET-lerz) People who move to a new land.

voyages (VOY-ij-iz) Journeys by water.

Index

Web Sites:

To find out more about whaleships and whaling, check out these Web sites:

www.kwm.org
www.whalingmuseum.org/whaling.htm